SPORTS CODING CONCEPTS

SPORTY LOOPING

Allyssa Loya

Lerner Publications ◆ Minneapolis

Lerner Publications Company
An imprint of Lerner Publishing Group, Inc.
241 First Avenue North
Minneapolis, MN 55401 USA

For reading levels and more information, look up this title at www.lernerbooks.com.

Main body text set in Mikado a Regular.
Typeface provided by HVD Fonts.

Library of Congress Cataloging-in-Publication Data

Names: Loya, Allyssa, author.
Title: Sporty looping / Allyssa Loya.
Description: Minneapolis : Lerner Publications, [2020] | Series: Sports coding concepts | Includes bibliographical references and index. | Audience: Age 7–9. | Audience: Grades K to 3.
Identifiers: LCCN 2019013117 (print) | LCCN 2019020224 (ebook) | ISBN 9781541583658 (eb pdf) | ISBN 9781541576940 (lb : alk. paper)
Subjects: LCSH: Loops (Computer programming)—Juvenile literature. | Sports—Juvenile literature.
Classification: LCC QA76.6115 (ebook) | LCC QA76.6115 .L694 2019 (print) | DDC 005.4/53—dc23

LC record available at https://lccn.loc.gov/2019013117

Manufactured in the United States of America
1-46713-47707-8/7/2019

Table of Contents

LET'S GET LOOPY!

Imagine you're coaching a robot basketball player. To give him instructions, you need to write lines of code. An algorithm is many lines of code put together. If the player needs to dribble five times, you might write him this algorithm:

dribble, dribble, dribble,
dribble, dribble

Or you could use a loop! A loop tells a computer to repeat a line of code a certain number of times. Instead of writing dribble five times, you could write this:

5(dribble)

Loops make coding quicker! Now it's your turn to practice. You will need paper and pencils for some of these activities.

DRILL, DRILL, DRILL

Exercising gets you ready for your games! You can use code to help you train.

Grab a partner and look at the exercise options on the next page. Then tell your partner a number and an exercise. For example, you could say 4(jumping jack). You are coding your partner with a loop! After your partner follows your instructions, switch and let your partner code you.

Exercise options:
jumping jack, somersault, push-up, cartwheel

SPLASH DASH

Swimmers, take your mark! The swimmers on the next page are racing through the pool.

First, count the number of sections left in their lanes. That's the number of strokes they need to finish their race. Then match each looped line of code to the correct swimmer. You can check your answer on page 29.

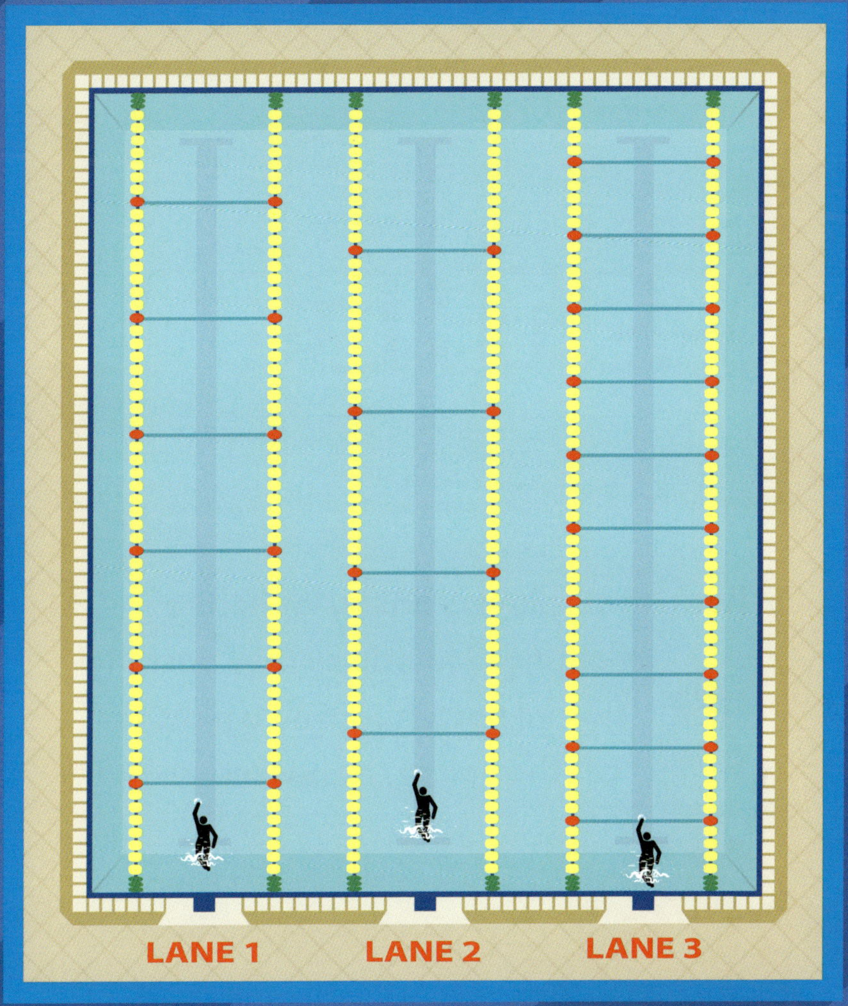

A. 10(stroke)

B. 6(stroke)

C. 4(stroke)

PASS THE BALL!

In basketball, players pass a lot before shooting. Sometimes they pass in a special pattern, called a play, to get the ball to the basket.

Check out the courts on page 11. To run the play, each player with an X needs to pass the ball. When the player with a ★ gets the ball, she'll shoot! Figure out the correct number of passes to finish the looped line of code. Go to page 29 to check your answer.

COURT
1

COURT
2

DO IT FOR LUCK

Before a game, some athletes do special moves for luck. A player may tap his chest or clap his hands. Think of these moves as lines of code that get him ready to play.

The next page shows three players doing their good-luck moves. On a piece of paper, write a looped line of code for each player. Use the moves listed below the players to write your code. Remember to use a number and parentheses. Go to page 29 to check your answer.

Good-luck moves:
clap, chest tap, jump,
skip, push-up

WATCH FOR MY SIGNAL

There's a runner on first and a runner on third. What's your next move? In the middle of a game, baseball coaches use hand signals to tell runners what to do.

Find a partner. Then look at the signal options on the next page. Write an algorithm with at least three different looped signals, like this:

3 (chest tap)
2 (clap)
5 (head nod)

Give the algorithm to your partner. Have your partner run, or act out, the algorithm. Switch jobs and try it a few more times. Get creative!

Signal options:
head nod, chest tap, clap, ear pull, stomp, knee tap, fist pump

SPEEDY LOOPS

Speed skaters can go as fast as a car! The skater on the next page needs to complete one lap around the track. He has to skate straight and then turn, repeating the moves in that order one time. You can use a loop to repeat multiple instructions. A loop with more than one instruction looks like this:

2(skate straight, turn)

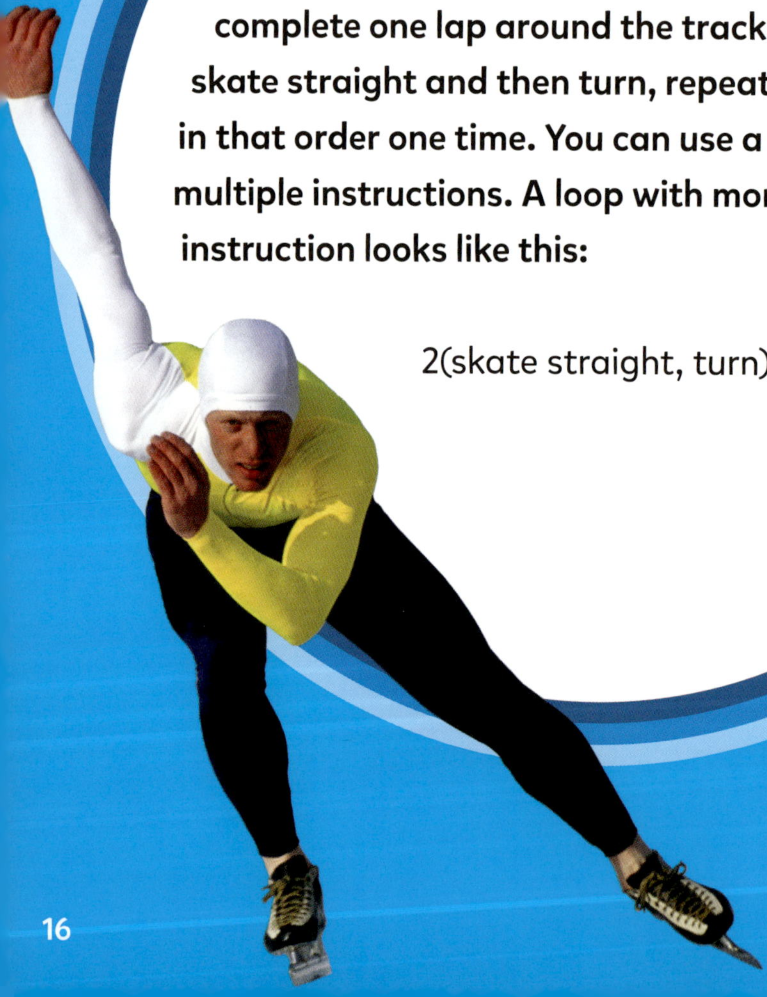

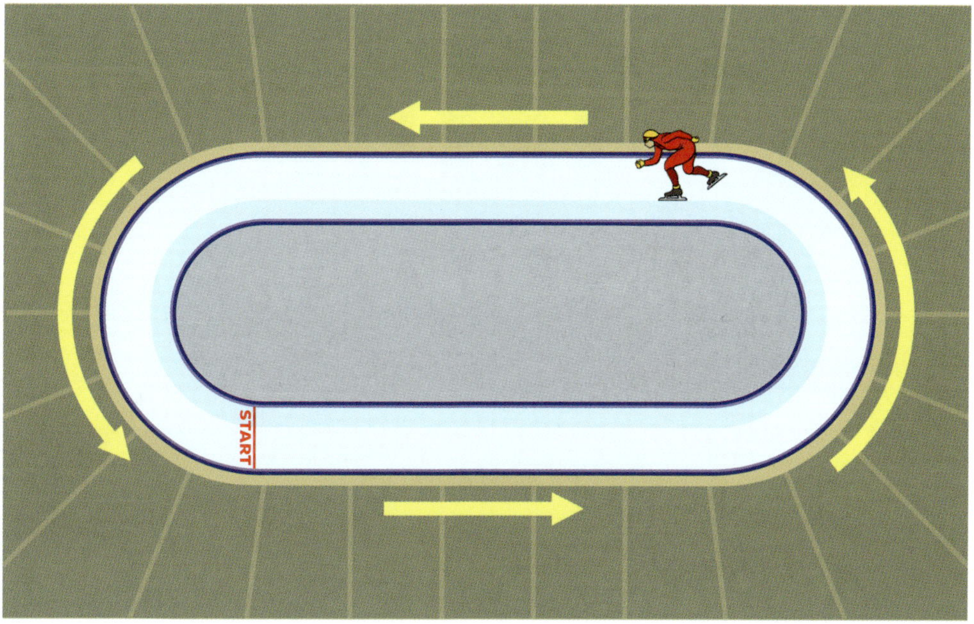

The skater's algorithm is **not** this:

2(skate straight) 2(turn)

That algorithm tells the skater to skate straight two times and then turn two times. If he ran that algorithm, he'd run right into the wall!

On a piece of paper, write a looped line of code for a skater that needs to go around the track **five** times. Check your answer on page 29.

PUTTING AROUND

Let's get golfing!

Grab a partner and three pieces of paper. Crumple two pieces of paper into balls. Then put the third piece of paper flat on the floor across the room. The flat piece of paper is your golf hole.

Take turns putting with your foot to get the ball into the hole. Count how many times you walk, aim, and putt. Then write an algorithm with loops that explains what you did. Remember that multiple instructions can go inside your loop.

In golf, the lowest score wins. So whoever has the shortest algorithm wins!

PRACTICE MAKES PERFECT

***Goooal!* In soccer, strikers usually take the shots. They practice shooting from different spots on the field. That way they'll be ready for a game!**

Look at the soccer field on page 21. Write an algorithm with loops to move the striker to all the Xs. Make sure to have a move and a kick inside your loop, like this: (↴, kick). The striker needs to practice running *and* shooting! Go to page 29 to check your answer.

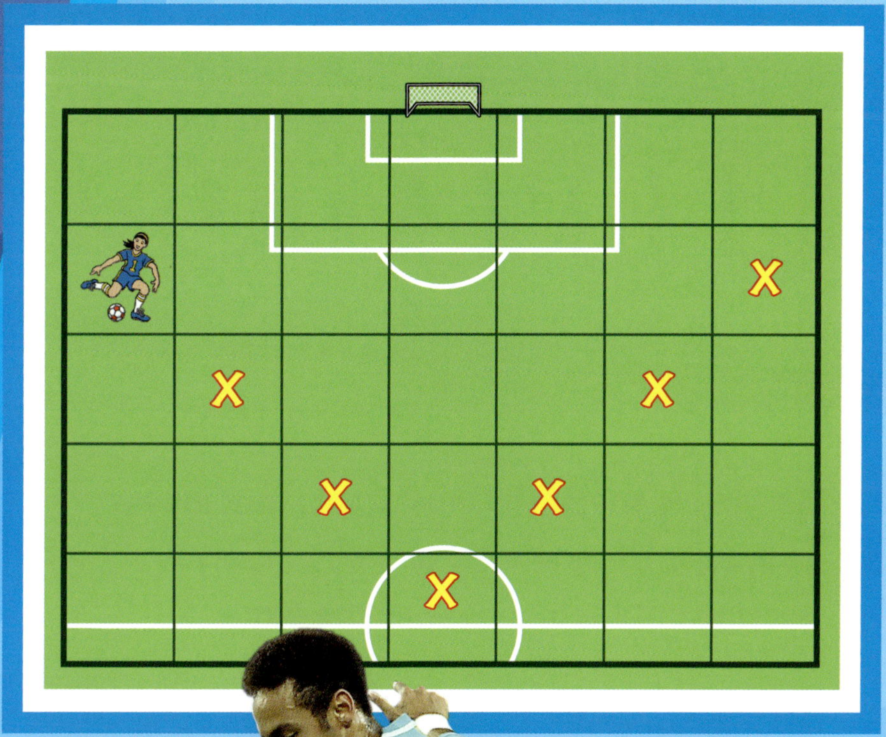

SERVE IT UP

Serving is one of the most important moves in tennis. The same player has to keep serving until someone wins the game.

Imagine a tennis player is coding herself to serve. She needs something called a do-until loop. Do-until loops keep going until something happens. Then they stop. On the next page is a do-until loop with a missing piece of code. On a separate sheet of paper, write what should stop the loop. Go to page 29 to check your answer.

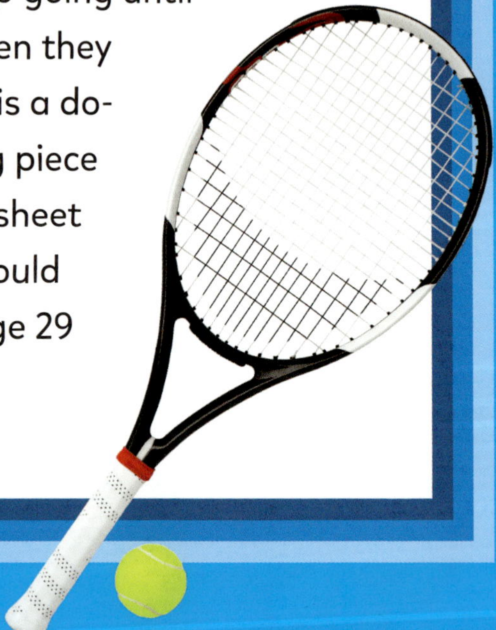

Do until ______________________________(serve)

A. someone wins the game
B. her opponent scores a point
C. she scores a point

SPEEDING AND WEAVING

Slalom skiers weave through sets of poles, or gates, until they get down the mountain. Their path down the slope is like an algorithm with a do-until loop.

On page 25 is a skier speeding down the mountain. She needs to go through every gate on her way down. When she lands on a square with a gate, she goes through it. On a piece of paper, write an algorithm to get the skier through the gates and across the finish line. Use the code below the mountain to write a do-until loop. Go to page 29 to check your answer.

Do until you're at the bottom(,   )

Code options:

OBSTACLES WON'T GET IN YOUR WAY!

Athletes have muscles, moves, and brains. But the thing they do most is train. Obstacle courses help you practice many different moves.

With a friend, look over the symbols on the next page. Draw one symbol each on different pieces of paper. Spread the papers on the floor around the room to make an obstacle course. Make lines to balance on, areas to jump over, and more!

Using everything you've learned about loops, write an algorithm to get your partner through the obstacle course.

For example, if these obstacles in this order:
X, O, –, X, O, –

your algorithm is:
2(jump over mud pit, duck under rope, balance on beam)!

<u>Symbol options</u>
<u>(or think of your own!):</u>

X: jump over mud pit

O: duck under rope

–: balance on beam

~: crawl through tunnel

Keep Coding!

Sports are all about practice! You run lots of laps, make the same passes, and take the same shots over and over. When you're playing a sport, think about how many times you do the same thing. How many times did you run across the court? How many times did you call your teammate's name? Now you can think of these moves as loops. How many shots did you miss until you made one? That's a do-until loop: do until you score(shoot)!

Before you know it, you'll start seeing loops everywhere—especially in sports!

Answer Key

Pages 8–9: Lane 1: B, Lane 2: C, Lane 3: A

Pages 10–11: Court 1: 2(pass), Court 2: 4(pass)

Pages 12–13: Player 1: 3(chest tap), Player 2: 5(jump), Player 3: 4(clap)

Pages 16–17: 10(skate straight, turn)

Pages 20–21: 3(↴, kick), 3(↱, kick)

Pages 22–23: Do until A. someone wins the game(serve)

Pages 24–25: do until you're at the bottom(↴, ⬐)

Glossary

algorithm: a group of instructions, made up of lines of code, that tells a computer what to do

code: instructions written for computers to follow

do-until loop: a loop that continues until something happens

dribble: in basketball, to bounce the ball on the floor as you move with the ball

loop: a line of code that tells a computer to repeat an instruction a certain number of times

pass: to move the ball or puck from one teammate to another

play: in some sports, a special pattern a team uses to move and pass the ball

putting: in golf, moving the ball into the hole with a small club

run: to start an algorithm

serve: to move or hit a ball and begin play

slalom: a skiing sport where the skier moves through sets of gates

Further Reading

Code.org: Getting Loopy
https://studio.code.org/s/course1/stage/12/puzzle/1

Coding: For Loops
https://www.flocabulary.com/unit/coding-for-loops/

Funk, Josh. *How to Code a Sandcastle*. New York: Viking, 2018.

Loya, Allyssa. *Sporty Algorithms*. Minneapolis: Lerner Publications, 2020.

Lyons, Heather, and Elizabeth Tweedale. *Learn to Program*. Minneapolis: Lerner Publications, 2017.

Scratch Jr.
https://www.scratchjr.org/

Index

Photo Acknowledgments

Image credits: Lachlan Cunningham/Getty Images, p. 4; Compassionate Eye Foundation/Steve Coleman/OJO Images Ltd/Getty Images, p. 5 (backboard); Suriyo Hmun Kaew/EyeEm/Getty Images, p. 5 (basketball 11); g&l images/Getty Images, p. 6; Javier Sánchez Mingorance/EyeEm/Getty Images, p. 7 (cartwheel); baona/Getty Images, p. 7 (somersault); Hero Images/Getty Images, pp. 7 (push-up), 27; mediaphotos/Getty Images, p. 8; PeopleImages/Getty Images, p. 9; Laura Westlund/Independent Picture Service, pp. 9 (illustration), 11, 13, 17, 21, 25; Rich von Biberstein/Icon Sportswire/Getty Images, p. 10; pat138241/Getty Images, p. 12; Rinek/Getty Images, p. 13; jpbcpa/Getty Images, p. 14; Robert D. Barnes/Getty Images, p. 15 (athlete); Jules Frazier/Getty Images, p. 15 (baseball); Jamie Squire/Getty Images, p. 16; Blend Images-Erik Isakson/Getty Images, p. 18 (athlete); Ponsulak Kunsub/EyeEm/Getty Images, p. 18 (golf ball); Danielle Reierson/EyeEm/Getty Images, p. 19; Lazi & Mellenthin/Getty Images, p. 20; Aurelien Meunier/Getty Images, p. 21; Creative Crop/Getty Images, p. 22; Simon M Bruty/Getty Images, p. 23; ninikas/Getty Images, p. 24; twinsterphoto/Getty Images, p. 26.

Cover: Ron Levine/Getty Images (basketball athlete), blackred/Getty Images (baseball glove), isitsharp/Getty Images (soccer athlete), Dan Thornberg/EyeEm/Getty Images (volleyball), Francesco Carta fotografo/Getty Images (football), noLimit46/Getty Images (background).

About the Author

Allyssa Loya is an elementary school librarian in North Texas and is the author of the Disney Coding Adventures series. Loya has two young boys. She is married to an IT manager, who is a perfect support system for her technological endeavors.